W9-CAL-235

PERSIAN Cats

by Joanne Mattern

CAPSTONE PRESS
a capstone imprint

Edge Books are published by Capstone Press,
151 Good Counsel Drive, P.O. Box 669, Mankato, Minnesota 56002.
www.capstonepub.com

Books published by Capstone Press are manufactured with paper
containing at least 10 percent post-consumer waste.

Library of Congress Cataloging-in-Publication Data
Mattern, Joanne, 1963–
  Persian cats / by Joanne Mattern.
      p. cm.—(Edge books. All about cats.)
  Includes bibliographical references and index.
  Summary: "Describes the history, physical features, and care of the Persian
      cat breed"—Provided by publisher.
  ISBN 978-1-4296-6634-3 (library binding)
  1. Persian cat—Juvenile literature. I. Title. II. Series.
  SF449.P4M382 2011
  636.8'32—dc22   2010039955

Editorial Credits
Angie Kaelberer and Carrie Braulick Sheely, editors; Heidi Thompson,
      designer; Wanda Winch, media researcher; Eric Manske,
      production specialist

Photo Credits
Corbis: Hulton-Deutsch Collection, 12; Photo by Fiona Green, 5, 7, 15, 19, 23,
      25, 27, 28; Shutterstock: Eric Isselée, 10, 21, Kirill Vorobyev, 16, Linn Currie,
      9, 11, Tamila Aspen (TAStudio), cover

Printed in the United States of America in Stevens Point, Wisconsin.
092010   005934WZS11

TABLE OF CONTENTS

Chapter 1

PRIZED PERSIANS

Persians are one of the best known and most popular cat breeds in the world. The Persian was the most popular breed in the Cat Fanciers' Association (CFA) from 2005 to 2009. The CFA is the largest cat registry in the world. The breed also topped the CFA popularity list often before 2005. Persians were one of the 10 most popular breeds in 2009 according to The International Cat Association (TICA).

When you consider Persians' traits, it is easy to see why these cats top popularity lists. A Persian's long, silky coat is one of its most attractive features. Persians also have unique facial features. The face has a flat, pushed-in appearance. Many people think the Persian's face gives it a sweet expression.

breed—a certain kind of animal within an animal group; breed also means to mate and raise a certain kind of animal

registry—an organization that keeps track of the ancestry for cats of a certain breed

 **FACT:** Many people say Persians communicate with their eyes instead of their voices.

The Persian's short nose helps people recognize the breed.

IS THE PERSIAN RIGHT FOR YOU?

Persians can live comfortably in a variety of households. Their quiet personalities make them best suited for calm households. But they can adapt to living in very active households with children. Persians also get along well with dogs and other cats.

In general, Persians are healthy cats that are easy to care for. But the Persian's long coat does need daily grooming to keep it healthy and attractive.

If you decide the Persian fits you, you can find one in several ways. Many people contact breeders or pet stores. Persians from these sources can cost several hundred dollars. However, breeders usually know the cat's history. Knowing the cat's history helps you be sure you are getting a healthy cat.

Breed rescue organizations and animal shelters can be less expensive places to get Persians. These organizations take care of pets until the animals can be placed in new homes. Rescue organizations may even have registered cats.

Shelters often have mixed-breed pets available instead of purebred animals such as the Persian. Many cat shows don't allow mixed-breed cats to compete. But a mixed-breed Persian can still make an excellent pet.

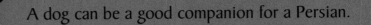

A dog can be a good companion for a Persian.

Chapter 2

PERSIAN HISTORY

The Persian is one of the oldest cat breeds. Much of the Persian's history is unknown. The breed's mysterious background has led people to tell stories about how it came about.

A MAGICAL LEGEND

One legend tells the story of a merchant who came across a group of robbers attacking a stranger. The merchant fought off the thieves and cared for the injured stranger.

After he recovered, the stranger told the merchant that he was a magician. He promised the merchant one wish in payment for saving his life. But the merchant did not want a wish. He was happy with his life. He told the magician that he liked to sit under the sparkling stars at night. He also said he liked to watch the smoke swirl from a crackling fire.

A popular legend about the first-ever Persian describes a cat similar in appearance to today's smoke-colored Persians.

The magician said that he could give the merchant the things he mentioned. The magician took a swirl of smoke, a spear of fire, and the light of two stars. The magician then created a cat with a fire-tipped tongue, smoke-gray fur, and sparkling eyes. The legend says that it was the first Persian cat.

THE REAL STORY

Most people think the Persian descended from longhaired Asian cats. Manuscripts and drawings from as early as 1684 BC show cats that look like Persians.

In the 1500s, European sailors and merchants often traveled to the Asian regions of Turkey and Persia. Today Persia is the country of Iran. These sailors and merchants brought longhaired cats back to Europe. The Turkish cats were called Angoras. The cats from Persia were called Persians. Both of these longhaired cats soon became popular with European royal families.

Turkish Angora

Persian

Early Angoras and Persians looked alike. But differences between the two breeds developed by the late 1800s. Persians were heavier than Angoras. Their coats were thicker. Persians also had larger heads and rounder eyes than Angoras.

FACT: Other cat breeds have also been kept and valued by royalty. These breeds include the Birman and the Siamese.

FROM EUROPE TO NORTH AMERICA

By 1903 Persians were recognized as a separate breed in Great Britain. But they were called longhairs instead of Persians.

After 1895 people brought Persians to North America from Europe. The Persian soon became very popular in shows and as pets.

In 1906 the CFA formed. A Persian named Molly Bond was one of the first cats registered. In 1914 the CFA formed a breed standard for Persians. This standard created color classes for Persians at shows. The standard was very similar to earlier British breed standards for Persians.

A breeder shows off her prize-winning Persian in 1935.

CHANGING LOOKS

Over time, cat breeders wanted the Persian to have a certain look. They carefully chose cats with specific traits that they wanted to continue in the breed. Because of this breeding, today's Persians look different than they once did. Modern Persians have shorter, more compact bodies than Persians of the early 1900s. Today's Persians also have thicker, longer fur than the original Persians did.

The biggest change in the Persian's appearance is in its face. Early Persians had wedge-shaped heads with long noses. But today's Persians have larger, more rounded heads. Their noses are also much shorter.

FACT: Today British people still call Persians longhairs or Persian longhairs.

breed standard—certain physical features in a breed that judges look for in a cat show

compact—short-bodied, solid, and without excess flesh

Chapter 3

SHORT AND SILKY

Persians are medium-sized cats. Adult Persians weigh 5 to 15 pounds (2.3 to 6.8 kilograms). Females are usually smaller than males.

Persians have short, stocky bodies that appear well-balanced. The chest is broad and deep. Short, thick legs and large, round paws add to the Persian's sturdy look.

COATS

Of all the Persian's features, the coat attracts the most attention. Persians have double coats of long, soft fur. The fur is thick and plush near the skin. This thick layer of fur is covered by lighter, silky fur. The outer coat can be 6 to 8 inches (15 to 20 centimeters) long.

A Persian's coat is heavier during the winter. During spring and summer, Persians shed this heavier coat.

A Persian also has a ruff around its neck and thick, flowing fur on its tail. The ruff comes to a point between the front legs.

ruff—a fringe or frill of long hairs growing around the neck of an animal

The Persian's long, heavy coat can add to the cat's stocky appearance.

solid Persian

tabby Persian

CFA COLOR DIVISIONS

Persians can be one of many colors and color combinations. The CFA divides Persians into seven color divisions for competition. These divisions include solid, shaded and smoke, tabby, and calico and bi-color. Parti-color, silver and golden, and Himalayan make up the other three color divisions.

SOLID, SHADED, AND SMOKED PERSIANS

Solid-colored Persians have undercoats and overcoats of one solid color. These colors may be white, black, blue, red, cream, chocolate, or lilac. Blue is a shade of gray. Lilac Persians have pink-gray coats.

Shaded Persians have white coats with colored tips at the end of each hair. These tips can be red, cream, black, or blue. Some shaded Persians have two or more colors of tips.

Smoke Persians may appear to be one color. But they actually have a white undercoat with a darker overcoat.

A RAINBOW OF COLORS

Many Persians have a mix of more than one color. Tabby Persians have coats with dark striped markings. Their coats can be silver, red, brown, blue, or other colors. Bi-color Persians have coats with patches of white and another solid color. Calico Persians are tri-colored cats with red, black, and white patches.

Parti-colored Persians' coats have patches of two or more colors. These color combinations include tortoiseshell, blue-cream, and lilac-cream. Tortoiseshell Persians have black or brown fur with red patches.

SILVER AND GOLDEN PERSIANS

Silver Persians have white coats. But each hair has a black tip. This coloring makes the cat's coat appear silver. Golden Persians also have black-tipped coats, but their coats are cream instead of white.

Silver and golden Persians have features not found in other Persians. These Persians' faces are less flat than those of other Persians. Silver and golden Persians also have thick black rims around their eyes.

 **FACT:** Blue and silver Persians were especially popular with early Persian owners in the United States.

Seal-point Himalayans have very dark brown colorpoints.

HIMALAYAN PERSIANS

Himalayan Persians resulted from mating Persian and Siamese cats. These cats have the compact body, long fur, and flat face of other Persians. They have colorpoints and blue eyes like Siamese cats.

The CFA considers Himalayans to be part of the Persian breed. But some other registries consider Himalayans to be a separate breed.

colorpoint—a pattern in which the ears, face, tail, and feet are darker than the base color

FACIAL FEATURES

Persians have large, round heads with full cheeks and broad jaws. The Persian's short, snub nose makes its face look flat. The nose has a dent called a break between the eyes. A Persian's small, rounded ears tilt slightly forward.

PERSONALITY

Persians are known for their calm, gentle personalities. They are among the quietest and least active of all cat breeds.

Persians also are friendly and affectionate. They seem to enjoy sitting on people's laps and being petted. They get along well with other animals.

FACT: Many cats enjoy climbing and jumping on top of objects high above the ground. But Persians seem to prefer being on the ground.

A Persian's large, rounded eyes are set wide apart.

Chapter 4

CARING FOR A PERSIAN

Persians are strong, healthy cats. With good care, Persians can live more than 15 years.

Like all cats, Persians should be kept indoors. Cats that roam outdoors have greater risks of developing diseases than indoor cats. Outdoor cats also face dangers from cars and other animals.

FEEDING

A balanced, nutritious diet will keep your Persian looking and feeling its best. Some cat owners feed dry food to their cats. This food has several benefits. It often is less expensive than other types of food. Dry food can help keep cats' teeth clean. It will not spoil if it is left in a dish.

Other owners feed moist, canned food to their cats. This type of food will spoil if it is left out too long. It should not be left out for more than an hour.

Cats need plenty of water to stay healthy. Keep your cat's water bowl filled with fresh, clean water.

FACT: Some owners feed both dry and moist food to their cats. This variety can help keep a cat from becoming bored with its diet.

Dry food can be left in a dish all day, allowing your cat to eat when it becomes hungry.

LITTER BOXES

Your Persian will need a litter box. Cats get rid of bodily waste in litter boxes. Most litter is made of clay. Litter may also be made from wood, corn, or other materials.

Keeping the box clean is important. Cats are clean animals and may refuse to use a dirty litter box. Clean the waste out of the box each day. Change the litter about every two weeks or when it appears wet or lumpy.

DENTAL CARE

Persians need regular dental care to protect their teeth and gums from decay. You should brush your cat's teeth at least weekly. Use a toothbrush made for cats or a soft cloth. Always use toothpaste made for cats. Toothpaste made for people can make cats sick.

litter—small bits of clay or other material used to absorb the waste of cats and other animals

Regular brushing will help keep your cat's teeth and gums healthy.

NAIL CARE

Like all cats, Persians need their nails trimmed every few weeks. Trimming helps reduce damage if cats scratch on furniture. It also protects cats from infections caused by ingrown nails. Ingrown nails occur when the claws grow into the pad or bottom of the paw. Many owners use trimmers made for pets. These trimmers are easy to handle and help prevent injury to cats while trimming.

GROOMING

Persians' long coats must be groomed with a wide-toothed metal comb daily to prevent mats. If mats do occur, owners should not cut them out with scissors. Cutting out mats can injure your cat or damage its coat. Instead, use a small-toothed comb to untangle mats.

Most cats do not need baths. But Persians' long coats should be bathed about once every three months. Owners should use a shampoo made for cats.

Persians' large eyes and flat faces allow tears to easily leak out of their eyes. Bacteria in tears can stain the cats' fur. To prevent these stains, clean around your Persian's eyes daily with a moistened tissue or cloth.

FACT: Scratching posts and boards can keep your cat from scratching on and damaging furniture.

bacteria—very small living things that can be found throughout nature; many bacteria are useful, but some cause disease

Brushing with a metal comb helps keep mats from forming in Persians' coats.

27

Vets use otoscopes to check cats' ears at checkups.

HEALTH CARE

Persians must visit a veterinarian at least once a year for checkups. The vet will give your cat any necessary vaccinations and check for signs of health problems. Persians can have some health problems. Cats often swallow fur as they groom their coats with their tongues. Because Persians have long hair, they are more likely to get hairballs.

vaccination—a shot of medicine that protects animals from disease

hairball—a ball of fur that lodges in a cat's stomach

If hairballs become too large, they can lodge in the cat's digestive system. A vet then may need to remove these hairballs. Regular combing is the best way to prevent hairballs.

Persians' short noses can cause breathing problems. These problems may lead to respiratory illnesses.

Persians can also develop a serious illness called polycystic kidney disease. This disease causes cats' kidneys to stop working properly. The disease is passed to kittens through their parents. Responsible breeders do tests for polycystic kidney disease before using cats for breeding.

All cats should be spayed or neutered by a vet unless their owners want to breed them. These surgeries make it impossible for cats to have kittens. Spaying and neutering helps control the pet population. It also helps prevent some diseases, such as cancer of the reproductive organs.

Regular visits to a vet are an important part of cat ownership. By working together, owners and vets can help Persians live long, healthy lives.

GLOSSARY

bacteria (bak-TEER-ee-uh)—very small living things that can be found throughout nature; many bacteria are useful, but some cause disease

breed (BREED)—a certain kind of animal within an animal group; breed also means to mate and raise a certain kind of animal

breed standard (BREED STAN-durd)—certain physical features in a breed that judges look for at a cat show

colorpoint (KUHL-ur-point)—a pattern in which the ears face, tail, and feet are darker than the base color

compact (kuhm-PAKT)—short-bodied, solid, and without excess flesh

hairball (HAIR-bawl)—a ball of fur that lodges in a cat's digestive system

litter (LIT-ur)—small bits of clay or other material used to absorb the waste of cats and other animals

mat (MAT)—tangled fur that forms a lump in the coat

registry (REH-juh-stree)—an organization that keeps track of the ancestry for cats of a certain breed

ruff (RUHF)—long hairs growing around an animal's neck

vaccination (vak-suh-NAY-shun)—a shot of medicine that protects animals from a disease

READ MORE

Britton, Tamara L. *Persian Cats.* Cats. Edina, Minn.: ABDO Publishing Company, 2011.

Markovics, Joyce L. *Persians: Longhaired Friends.* Cat-ographies. New York: Bearport, 2011.

Mattern, Joanne. *Siamese Cats.* All About Cats. Mankato, Minn.: Capstone Press, 2011.

Wilsdon, Christina. *Cats.* Amazing Animals. Pleasantville, N.Y.: Gareth Stevens Pub., 2009.

INTERNET SITES

FactHound offers a safe, fun way to find Internet sites related to this book. All of the sites on FactHound have been researched by our staff.

Here's all you do:

Visit *www.facthound.com*

Type in this code: 9781429666343

Check out projects, games and lots more at
www.capstonekids.com

INDEX